The Art of Gratitude
Journal

**A Journey
to the
Power of Peace**

Donna
Piromalli

Name: _____

Date: _____

Donna Piromalli Books & Coaching Programs

Books
More Than Just a Hairdresser - Book
More Than Just a Hairdresser - Workbook
The Art of Gratitude - Journal

Programs

THE ART OF LIVING PROGRAM
An individual program tailored to your specific needs for personal or professional growth or both.

THE ART OF POSITIVE CULTURE
A tailored program to address the needs of your business, group dymanics and your work environment.

For More Information Please Visit
www.DonnaPiromalli.com
www.griffithcounselling.com

Copyright © 2020 by Donna Piromalli

All rights reserved. This book may not be reproduced in whole or in part, by any means, without the written consent of the publisher. For permission requests, write to the publisher, addressed "Attention Permissions Coordinator" at the address below.

Donna Piromalli
P.O.BOX 1152
Griffith, NSW 2680
Australia

The Art of Gratitude

Gratitude is defined by the Wester Dictionary as the quality of being thankful; readiness to show appreciation for and to return kindness. In short, it is a recognition of the emotion of thankfulness. Gratitude has the unique ability to shift our thoughts toward a positive, empowering feeling of good.

I tell my coaching clients repeatedly that what you focus on expands. That means when your mind is focused on gratitude, it does not allow negative emotions or feelings to derail or consume your thoughts. There are times in everyone's life that things go wrong, bad events happen and the world spins beyond your control. However, even then, you can find things to be grateful for that will allow you to regain control of your life. Whether it be the people in your life or the smallest kernel of hope you have left, gratitude can lift you out of the negative emotions and give you an ability to accomplish great things.

This book is separated into four sections of 13 weeks each. Every day you can list those things you are grateful for as well as the special things you experience each week. Every 13 weeks, there is space to look back and remember those things that meant the most to you. At the end of 52 weeks, you can review the full year and think about how far you have come in your own gratitude journey during that time.

Cultivating a habitual mindset of gratitude has tremendous power to allow you to fully enjoy your life. It gives you both a perspective of your past, more joy for today and hope for the future. My wish for you is that you make this a vital part of your personal growth journey.

Donna Piromalli

The Art of Gratitude

Acknowledging the good that you already have in your life is the foundation for all abundance.
Eckhart Tolle

DATE: _____
I am so happy and grateful now that . . .
1. _____
2. _____
3. _____
4. _____

DATE: _____
I am so happy and grateful now that . . .
1. _____
2. _____
3. _____
4. _____

DATE: _____
I am so happy and grateful now that . . .
1. _____
2. _____
3. _____
4. _____

DATE: _____
I am so happy and grateful now that . . .
1. _____
2. _____
3. _____
4. _____

DATE: _____   Week 1 - Week 13

I am so happy and grateful now that . . .

1. _____
2. _____
3. _____
4. _____

DATE: _____

I am so happy and grateful now that . . .

1. _____
2. _____
3. _____
4. _____

DATE: _____

I am so happy and grateful now that . . .

1. _____
2. _____
3. _____
4. _____

Things that touched my heart the most this week:

_____
_____
_____
_____
_____
_____
_____
_____
_____

The Art of Gratitude

Gratitude is the healthiest of all human emotions. The more you recognize and express gratitude for the things you have, the more things you will have to express gratitude for.
Zig Ziglar

DATE: _____
I am so happy and grateful now that . . .
1. _____
2. _____
3. _____
4. _____

DATE: _____
I am so happy and grateful now that . . .
1. _____
2. _____
3. _____
4. _____

DATE: _____
I am so happy and grateful now that . . .
1. _____
2. _____
3. _____
4. _____

DATE: _____
I am so happy and grateful now that . . .
1. _____
2. _____
3. _____
4. _____

DATE: _____

Week 1 - Week 13

I am so happy and grateful now that . . .

1. _____
2. _____
3. _____
4. _____

DATE: _____

I am so happy and grateful now that . . .

1. _____
2. _____
3. _____
4. _____

DATE: _____

I am so happy and grateful now that . . .

1. _____
2. _____
3. _____
4. _____

Things that touched my heart the most this week:

_____
_____
_____
_____
_____
_____
_____
_____

The Art of Gratitude

As we express our gratitude, we must never forget that the highest appreciation is not to utter words, but to live by them.
John F. Kennedy

DATE: _____
I am so happy and grateful now that . . .
1. _____
2. _____
3. _____
4. _____

DATE: _____
I am so happy and grateful now that . . .
1. _____
2. _____
3. _____
4. _____

DATE: _____
I am so happy and grateful now that . . .
1. _____
2. _____
3. _____
4. _____

DATE: _____
I am so happy and grateful now that . . .
1. _____
2. _____
3. _____
4. _____

DATE: _____   Week 1 - Week 13

I am so happy and grateful now that . . .

1. _____
2. _____
3. _____
4. _____

DATE: _____

I am so happy and grateful now that . . .

1. _____
2. _____
3. _____
4. _____

DATE: _____

I am so happy and grateful now that . . .

1. _____
2. _____
3. _____
4. _____

Things that touched my heart the most this week:

_____
_____
_____
_____
_____
_____
_____
_____

The Art of Gratitude

Happiness cannot be traveled to, owned, earned, worn or consumed. Happiness is the spiritual experience of living every minute with love, grace and gratitude.
Denis Waitley

DATE: _____
I am so happy and grateful now that . . .
1. _____
2. _____
3. _____
4. _____

DATE: _____
I am so happy and grateful now that . . .
1. _____
2. _____
3. _____
4. _____

DATE: _____
I am so happy and grateful now that . . .
1. _____
2. _____
3. _____
4. _____

DATE: _____
I am so happy and grateful now that . . .
1. _____
2. _____
3. _____
4. _____

DATE: _____ Week 1 - Week 13

I am so happy and grateful now that . . .

1. _____
2. _____
3. _____
4. _____

DATE: _____

I am so happy and grateful now that . . .

1. _____
2. _____
3. _____
4. _____

DATE: _____

I am so happy and grateful now that . . .

1. _____
2. _____
3. _____
4. _____

Things that touched my heart the most this week:

_____
_____
_____
_____
_____
_____
_____
_____
_____

The Art of Gratitude

Let us be grateful to people who make us happy; they are the charming gardeners who make our souls blossom.
Marcel Proust

DATE: _____
I am so happy and grateful now that . . .
1. _____
2. _____
3. _____
4. _____

DATE: _____
I am so happy and grateful now that . . .
1. _____
2. _____
3. _____
4. _____

DATE: _____
I am so happy and grateful now that . . .
1. _____
2. _____
3. _____
4. _____

DATE: _____
I am so happy and grateful now that . . .
1. _____
2. _____
3. _____
4. _____

DATE: _____   Week 1 - Week 13
I am so happy and grateful now that . . .

1. _____
2. _____
3. _____
4. _____

DATE: _____
I am so happy and grateful now that . . .

1. _____
2. _____
3. _____
4. _____

DATE: _____
I am so happy and grateful now that . . .

1. _____
2. _____
3. _____
4. _____

Things that touched my heart the most this week:

_____
_____
_____
_____
_____
_____
_____
_____

The Art of Gratitude

Gratitude bestows reverence, allowing us to encounter everyday epiphanies, those transcendent moments of awe that change forever how we experience life and the world.
John Milton

DATE: _____
I am so happy and grateful now that . . .
1. _____
2. _____
3. _____
4. _____

DATE: _____
I am so happy and grateful now that . . .
1. _____
2. _____
3. _____
4. _____

DATE: _____
I am so happy and grateful now that . . .
1. _____
2. _____
3. _____
4. _____

DATE: _____
I am so happy and grateful now that . . .
1. _____
2. _____
3. _____
4. _____

DATE: _____   Week 1 - Week 13

I am so happy and grateful now that . . .

1. _____
2. _____
3. _____
4. _____

DATE: _____

I am so happy and grateful now that . . .

1. _____
2. _____
3. _____
4. _____

DATE: _____

I am so happy and grateful now that . . .

1. _____
2. _____
3. _____
4. _____

Things that touched my heart the most this week:

_____
_____
_____
_____
_____
_____
_____
_____

The Art of Gratitude

Nothing new can come into your life unless you are grateful for what you already have.
Michael Bernard

DATE: _____
I am so happy and grateful now that . . .
1. _____
2. _____
3. _____
4. _____

DATE: _____
I am so happy and grateful now that . . .
1. _____
2. _____
3. _____
4. _____

DATE: _____
I am so happy and grateful now that . . .
1. _____
2. _____
3. _____
4. _____

DATE: _____
I am so happy and grateful now that . . .
1. _____
2. _____
3. _____
4. _____

DATE: _____   Week 1 - Week 13
I am so happy and grateful now that . . .
1. _____
2. _____
3. _____
4. _____

DATE: _____
I am so happy and grateful now that . . .
1. _____
2. _____
3. _____
4. _____

DATE: _____
I am so happy and grateful now that . . .
1. _____
2. _____
3. _____
4. _____

Things that touched my heart the most this week:
_____
_____
_____
_____
_____
_____
_____
_____
_____

The Art of Gratitude

Gratitude turns what we have into enough.
Aesop

DATE: _____
I am so happy and grateful now that . . .
1. _____
2. _____
3. _____
4. _____

DATE: _____
I am so happy and grateful now that . . .
1. _____
2. _____
3. _____
4. _____

DATE: _____
I am so happy and grateful now that . . .
1. _____
2. _____
3. _____
4. _____

DATE: _____
I am so happy and grateful now that . . .
1. _____
2. _____
3. _____
4. _____

DATE: _____   **Week 1 - Week 13**

I am so happy and grateful now that . . .

1. _____
2. _____
3. _____
4. _____

DATE: _____

I am so happy and grateful now that . . .

1. _____
2. _____
3. _____
4. _____

DATE: _____

I am so happy and grateful now that . . .

1. _____
2. _____
3. _____
4. _____

Things that touched my heart the most this week:

_____
_____
_____
_____
_____
_____
_____
_____
_____

The Art of Gratitude

When we give cheerfully and accept gratefully, everyone is blessed.
Maya Angelou

DATE: _____
I am so happy and grateful now that . . .
1. _____
2. _____
3. _____
4. _____

DATE: _____
I am so happy and grateful now that . . .
1. _____
2. _____
3. _____
4. _____

DATE: _____
I am so happy and grateful now that . . .
1. _____
2. _____
3. _____
4. _____

DATE: _____
I am so happy and grateful now that . . .
1. _____
2. _____
3. _____
4. _____

DATE: _____ **Week 1 - Week 13**

I am so happy and grateful now that . . .

1. _____
2. _____
3. _____
4. _____

DATE: _____

I am so happy and grateful now that . . .

1. _____
2. _____
3. _____
4. _____

DATE: _____

I am so happy and grateful now that . . .

1. _____
2. _____
3. _____
4. _____

Things that touched my heart the most this week:

_____
_____
_____
_____
_____
_____
_____
_____

The Art of Gratitude

Gratitude is a quality similar to electricity: it must be produced and discharged and used up in order to exist at all.
William Faulkner

DATE: _____
I am so happy and grateful now that . . .
1. _____
2. _____
3. _____
4. _____

DATE: _____
I am so happy and grateful now that . . .
1. _____
2. _____
3. _____
4. _____

DATE: _____
I am so happy and grateful now that . . .
1. _____
2. _____
3. _____
4. _____

DATE: _____
I am so happy and grateful now that . . .
1. _____
2. _____
3. _____
4. _____

DATE: _____   Week 1 - Week 13

I am so happy and grateful now that . . .

1. _____
2. _____
3. _____
4. _____

DATE: _____

I am so happy and grateful now that . . .

1. _____
2. _____
3. _____
4. _____

DATE: _____

I am so happy and grateful now that . . .

1. _____
2. _____
3. _____
4. _____

Things that touched my heart the most this week:

_____
_____
_____
_____
_____
_____
_____
_____

The Art of Gratitude

Gratitude is an opener of locked-up blessings.
Marianne Williamson

DATE: _____
I am so happy and grateful now that . . .
1. _____
2. _____
3. _____
4. _____

DATE: _____
I am so happy and grateful now that . . .
1. _____
2. _____
3. _____
4. _____

DATE: _____
I am so happy and grateful now that . . .
1. _____
2. _____
3. _____
4. _____

DATE: _____
I am so happy and grateful now that . . .
1. _____
2. _____
3. _____
4. _____

DATE: _____   Week 1 - Week 13

I am so happy and grateful now that . . .

1. _____
2. _____
3. _____
4. _____

DATE: _____

I am so happy and grateful now that . . .

1. _____
2. _____
3. _____
4. _____

DATE: _____

I am so happy and grateful now that . . .

1. _____
2. _____
3. _____
4. _____

Things that touched my heart the most this week:

_____
_____
_____
_____
_____
_____
_____
_____
_____

The Art of Gratitude

Gratitude is a currency that we can mint for ourselves, and spend without fear of bankruptcy.
Fred De Witt Van Amburgh

DATE: _____
I am so happy and grateful now that . . .
1. _____
2. _____
3. _____
4. _____

DATE: _____
I am so happy and grateful now that . . .
1. _____
2. _____
3. _____
4. _____

DATE: _____
I am so happy and grateful now that . . .
1. _____
2. _____
3. _____
4. _____

DATE: _____
I am so happy and grateful now that . . .
1. _____
2. _____
3. _____
4. _____

DATE: _____   Week 1 - Week 13

I am so happy and grateful now that . . .

1. _____
2. _____
3. _____
4. _____

DATE: _____

I am so happy and grateful now that . . .

1. _____
2. _____
3. _____
4. _____

DATE: _____

I am so happy and grateful now that . . .

1. _____
2. _____
3. _____
4. _____

Things that touched my heart the most this week:

_____
_____
_____
_____
_____
_____
_____
_____

The Art of Gratitude

Gratitude is the ability to experience life as a gift. It liberates us from the prison of self-preoccupation.
John Ortberg

DATE: _____
I am so happy and grateful now that . . .
1. _____
2. _____
3. _____
4. _____

DATE: _____
I am so happy and grateful now that . . .
1. _____
2. _____
3. _____
4. _____

DATE: _____
I am so happy and grateful now that . . .
1. _____
2. _____
3. _____
4. _____

DATE: _____
I am so happy and grateful now that . . .
1. _____
2. _____
3. _____
4. _____

DATE: _____ Week 1 - Week 13

I am so happy and grateful now that . . .

1. _____
2. _____
3. _____
4. _____

DATE: _____

I am so happy and grateful now that . . .

1. _____
2. _____
3. _____
4. _____

DATE: _____

I am so happy and grateful now that . . .

1. _____
2. _____
3. _____
4. _____

Things that touched my heart the most this week:

_____
_____
_____
_____
_____
_____
_____
_____

The Art of Gratitude

Date:_____

Review the last 13 weeks of this journal. List the things you are most grateful to have experienced during this time.

1. _____
_____
2. _____
_____
3. _____
_____
4. _____
_____
5. _____
_____
6. _____
_____
7. _____
_____
8. _____
_____
9. _____
_____
10. _____
_____
11. _____
_____
12. _____
_____

The Art of Gratitude

Date:_____

How do you feel keeping a gratitude journal has impacted the last few months of your life?

_____
_____
_____
_____
_____
_____
_____
_____
_____
_____
_____
_____
_____
_____
_____
_____
_____
_____
_____
_____
_____
_____
_____
_____

The Art of Gratitude

Gratitude is not only the greatest of virtues but the parent of all others.
Marcus Tellius Cicero

DATE: _____
I am so happy and grateful now that . . .
1. _____
2. _____
3. _____
4. _____

DATE: _____
I am so happy and grateful now that . . .
1. _____
2. _____
3. _____
4. _____

DATE: _____
I am so happy and grateful now that . . .
1. _____
2. _____
3. _____
4. _____

DATE: _____
I am so happy and grateful now that . . .
1. _____
2. _____
3. _____
4. _____

DATE: _____

Week 14 - Week 26

I am so happy and grateful now that . . .

1. _____
2. _____
3. _____
4. _____

DATE: _____

I am so happy and grateful now that . . .

1. _____
2. _____
3. _____
4. _____

DATE: _____

I am so happy and grateful now that . . .

1. _____
2. _____
3. _____
4. _____

Things that touched my heart the most this week:

_____
_____
_____
_____
_____
_____
_____
_____

The Art of Gratitude

Our favorite attitude should be gratitude.
Zig Ziglar

DATE: _____
I am so happy and grateful now that . . .
1. _____
2. _____
3. _____
4. _____

DATE: _____
I am so happy and grateful now that . . .
1. _____
2. _____
3. _____
4. _____

DATE: _____
I am so happy and grateful now that . . .
1. _____
2. _____
3. _____
4. _____

DATE: _____
I am so happy and grateful now that . . .
1. _____
2. _____
3. _____
4. _____

DATE: _____

Week 14 - Week 26

I am so happy and grateful now that . . .

1. _____
2. _____
3. _____
4. _____

DATE: _____

I am so happy and grateful now that . . .

1. _____
2. _____
3. _____
4. _____

DATE: _____

I am so happy and grateful now that . . .

1. _____
2. _____
3. _____
4. _____

Things that touched my heart the most this week:

_____
_____
_____
_____
_____
_____
_____
_____
_____

The Art of Gratitude

*When you are grateful, fear disappears
and abundance appears.*
Tony Robbins

DATE: _____
I am so happy and grateful now that . . .
1. _____
2. _____
3. _____
4. _____

DATE: _____
I am so happy and grateful now that . . .
1. _____
2. _____
3. _____
4. _____

DATE: _____
I am so happy and grateful now that . . .
1. _____
2. _____
3. _____
4. _____

DATE: _____
I am so happy and grateful now that . . .
1. _____
2. _____
3. _____
4. _____

DATE: _____   Week 14 - Week 26

I am so happy and grateful now that . . .

1. _____
2. _____
3. _____
4. _____

DATE: _____

I am so happy and grateful now that . . .

1. _____
2. _____
3. _____
4. _____

DATE: _____

I am so happy and grateful now that . . .

1. _____
2. _____
3. _____
4. _____

Things that touched my heart the most this week:

_____
_____
_____
_____
_____
_____
_____
_____

The Art of Gratitude

What separates privilege from entitlement is gratitude.
Brené Brown

DATE: _____
I am so happy and grateful now that . . .
1. _____
2. _____
3. _____
4. _____

DATE: _____
I am so happy and grateful now that . . .
1. _____
2. _____
3. _____
4. _____

DATE: _____
I am so happy and grateful now that . . .
1. _____
2. _____
3. _____
4. _____

DATE: _____
I am so happy and grateful now that . . .
1. _____
2. _____
3. _____
4. _____

DATE: _____ **Week 14 – Week 26**
I am so happy and grateful now that . . .
1. _____
2. _____
3. _____
4. _____

DATE: _____
I am so happy and grateful now that . . .
1. _____
2. _____
3. _____
4. _____

DATE: _____
I am so happy and grateful now that . . .
1. _____
2. _____
3. _____
4. _____

Things that touched my heart the most this week:
_____
_____
_____
_____
_____
_____
_____
_____

The Art of Gratitude

Wear gratitude like a cloak and it will feed every corner of your life.
Rumi

DATE: _____
I am so happy and grateful now that . . .
1. _____
2. _____
3. _____
4. _____

DATE: _____
I am so happy and grateful now that . . .
1. _____
2. _____
3. _____
4. _____

DATE: _____
I am so happy and grateful now that . . .
1. _____
2. _____
3. _____
4. _____

DATE: _____
I am so happy and grateful now that . . .
1. _____
2. _____
3. _____
4. _____

DATE: _____ Week 14 - Week 26

I am so happy and grateful now that . . .

1. _____
2. _____
3. _____
4. _____

DATE: _____

I am so happy and grateful now that . . .

1. _____
2. _____
3. _____
4. _____

DATE: _____

I am so happy and grateful now that . . .

1. _____
2. _____
3. _____
4. _____

Things that touched my heart the most this week:

_____
_____
_____
_____
_____
_____
_____
_____

The Art of Gratitude

*Appreciation is the purest vibration that
exists on the planet today.*
Abraham Hicks

DATE: _____
I am so happy and grateful now that . . .
1. _____
2. _____
3. _____
4. _____

DATE: _____
I am so happy and grateful now that . . .
1. _____
2. _____
3. _____
4. _____

DATE: _____
I am so happy and grateful now that . . .
1. _____
2. _____
3. _____
4. _____

DATE: _____
I am so happy and grateful now that . . .
1. _____
2. _____
3. _____
4. _____

DATE: _____   **Week 14 - Week 26**
I am so happy and grateful now that . . .

1. _____
2. _____
3. _____
4. _____

DATE: _____
I am so happy and grateful now that . . .

1. _____
2. _____
3. _____
4. _____

DATE: _____
I am so happy and grateful now that . . .

1. _____
2. _____
3. _____
4. _____

Things that touched my heart the most this week:

_____
_____
_____
_____
_____
_____
_____
_____
_____

The Art of Gratitude

Gratitude can transform common days into thanksgivings, turn routine jobs into joy, and change ordinary opportunities into blessings.
William Arthur Ward

DATE: _____
I am so happy and grateful now that . . .
1. _____
2. _____
3. _____
4. _____

DATE: _____
I am so happy and grateful now that . . .
1. _____
2. _____
3. _____
4. _____

DATE: _____
I am so happy and grateful now that . . .
1. _____
2. _____
3. _____
4. _____

DATE: _____
I am so happy and grateful now that . . .
1. _____
2. _____
3. _____
4. _____

DATE: _____   Week 14 - Week 26

I am so happy and grateful now that . . .

1. _____
2. _____
3. _____
4. _____

DATE: _____

I am so happy and grateful now that . . .

1. _____
2. _____
3. _____
4. _____

DATE: _____

I am so happy and grateful now that . . .

1. _____
2. _____
3. _____
4. _____

Things that touched my heart the most this week:

_____
_____
_____
_____
_____
_____
_____
_____

The Art of Gratitude

To speak gratitude is courteous and pleasant, to enact gratitude is generous and noble, but to live gratitude is to touch Heaven.
Johannes A. Gaertner

DATE: _____
I am so happy and grateful now that . . .
1. _____
2. _____
3. _____
4. _____

DATE: _____
I am so happy and grateful now that . . .
1. _____
2. _____
3. _____
4. _____

DATE: _____
I am so happy and grateful now that . . .
1. _____
2. _____
3. _____
4. _____

DATE: _____
I am so happy and grateful now that . . .
1. _____
2. _____
3. _____
4. _____

DATE: _____   Week 14 - Week 26

I am so happy and grateful now that . . .

1. _____
2. _____
3. _____
4. _____

DATE: _____

I am so happy and grateful now that . . .

1. _____
2. _____
3. _____
4. _____

DATE: _____

I am so happy and grateful now that . . .

1. _____
2. _____
3. _____
4. _____

Things that touched my heart the most this week:

_____
_____
_____
_____
_____
_____
_____
_____

The Art of Gratitude

The thankful receiver bears a plentiful harvest.
William Blake

DATE: _____
I am so happy and grateful now that . . .
1. _____
2. _____
3. _____
4. _____

DATE: _____
I am so happy and grateful now that . . .
1. _____
2. _____
3. _____
4. _____

DATE: _____
I am so happy and grateful now that . . .
1. _____
2. _____
3. _____
4. _____

DATE: _____
I am so happy and grateful now that . . .
1. _____
2. _____
3. _____
4. _____

DATE: _____

Week 14 - Week 26

I am so happy and grateful now that . . .

1. _____
2. _____
3. _____
4. _____

DATE: _____

I am so happy and grateful now that . . .

1. _____
2. _____
3. _____
4. _____

DATE: _____

I am so happy and grateful now that . . .

1. _____
2. _____
3. _____
4. _____

Things that touched my heart the most this week:

_____
_____
_____
_____
_____
_____
_____
_____
_____

The Art of Gratitude

Let gratitude be the pillow upon which you kneel to say your nightly prayer. And let faith be the bridge you build to overcome evil and welcome good.
Maya Angelou

DATE: _____
I am so happy and grateful now that . . .
1. _____
2. _____
3. _____
4. _____

DATE: _____
I am so happy and grateful now that . . .
1. _____
2. _____
3. _____
4. _____

DATE: _____
I am so happy and grateful now that . . .
1. _____
2. _____
3. _____
4. _____

DATE: _____
I am so happy and grateful now that . . .
1. _____
2. _____
3. _____
4. _____

Week 14 - Week 26

DATE: _____
I am so happy and grateful now that . . .
1. _____
2. _____
3. _____
4. _____

DATE: _____
I am so happy and grateful now that . . .
1. _____
2. _____
3. _____
4. _____

DATE: _____
I am so happy and grateful now that . . .
1. _____
2. _____
3. _____
4. _____

Things that touched my heart the most this week:
_____
_____
_____
_____
_____
_____
_____
_____

The Art of Gratitude

Joy is the simplest form of gratitude.
Karl Barth

DATE: _____
I am so happy and grateful now that . . .
1. _____
2. _____
3. _____
4. _____

DATE: _____
I am so happy and grateful now that . . .
1. _____
2. _____
3. _____
4. _____

DATE: _____
I am so happy and grateful now that . . .
1. _____
2. _____
3. _____
4. _____

DATE: _____
I am so happy and grateful now that . . .
1. _____
2. _____
3. _____
4. _____

Week 14 - Week 26

DATE: _____
I am so happy and grateful now that . . .
1. _____
2. _____
3. _____
4. _____

DATE: _____
I am so happy and grateful now that . . .
1. _____
2. _____
3. _____
4. _____

DATE: _____
I am so happy and grateful now that . . .
1. _____
2. _____
3. _____
4. _____

Things that touched my heart the most this week:

_____
_____
_____
_____
_____
_____
_____
_____

The Art of Gratitude

Gratitude helps you to grow and expand; gratitude brings joy and laughter into your life and into the lives of all those around you.
Eileen Caddy

DATE: _____
I am so happy and grateful now that . . .
1. _____
2. _____
3. _____
4. _____

DATE: _____
I am so happy and grateful now that . . .
1. _____
2. _____
3. _____
4. _____

DATE: _____
I am so happy and grateful now that . . .
1. _____
2. _____
3. _____
4. _____

DATE: _____
I am so happy and grateful now that . . .
1. _____
2. _____
3. _____
4. _____

DATE: _____   Week 14 - Week 26
I am so happy and grateful now that . . .
1. _____
2. _____
3. _____
4. _____

DATE: _____
I am so happy and grateful now that . . .
1. _____
2. _____
3. _____
4. _____

DATE: _____
I am so happy and grateful now that . . .
1. _____
2. _____
3. _____
4. _____

Things that touched my heart the most this week:
_____
_____
_____
_____
_____
_____
_____
_____

The Art of Gratitude

*It is impossible to feel grateful and depressed
in the same moment.*
Naomi Williams

DATE: _____
I am so happy and grateful now that . . .
1. _____
2. _____
3. _____
4. _____

DATE: _____
I am so happy and grateful now that . . .
1. _____
2. _____
3. _____
4. _____

DATE: _____
I am so happy and grateful now that . . .
1. _____
2. _____
3. _____
4. _____

DATE: _____
I am so happy and grateful now that . . .
1. _____
2. _____
3. _____
4. _____

Week 14 – Week 26

DATE: _____
I am so happy and grateful now that . . .
1. _____
2. _____
3. _____
4. _____

DATE: _____
I am so happy and grateful now that . . .
1. _____
2. _____
3. _____
4. _____

DATE: _____
I am so happy and grateful now that . . .
1. _____
2. _____
3. _____
4. _____

Things that touched my heart the most this week:
_____
_____
_____
_____
_____
_____
_____
_____

The Art of Gratitude

Date:_____

Review the last 13 weeks of this journal. List the things you are most grateful to have experienced during this time.

1. _____
_____
2. _____
_____
3. _____
_____
4. _____
_____
5. _____
_____
6. _____
_____
7. _____
_____
8. _____
_____
9. _____
_____
10. _____
_____
11. _____
_____
12. _____
_____

The Art of Gratitude

Date:_____

How do you feel keeping a gratitude journal has impacted the last few months of your life?
_____
_____
_____
_____
_____
_____
_____
_____
_____
_____
_____
_____
_____
_____
_____
_____
_____
_____
_____
_____
_____
_____
_____
_____
_____

The Art of Gratitude

*It is impossible to feel grateful and depressed
in the same moment.*
Naomi Williams

DATE: _____
I am so happy and grateful now that . . .
1. _____
2. _____
3. _____
4. _____

DATE: _____
I am so happy and grateful now that . . .
1. _____
2. _____
3. _____
4. _____

DATE: _____
I am so happy and grateful now that . . .
1. _____
2. _____
3. _____
4. _____

DATE: _____
I am so happy and grateful now that . . .
1. _____
2. _____
3. _____
4. _____

DATE: _____

Week 27 - Week 39

I am so happy and grateful now that . . .

1. _____
2. _____
3. _____
4. _____

DATE: _____

I am so happy and grateful now that . . .

1. _____
2. _____
3. _____
4. _____

DATE: _____

I am so happy and grateful now that . . .

1. _____
2. _____
3. _____
4. _____

Things that touched my heart the most this week:

_____
_____
_____
_____
_____
_____
_____
_____

The Art of Gratitude

What you focus on expands, and when you focus on the goodness in your life, you create more of it. Opportunities, relationships, even money flowed my way when I learned to be grateful no matter what happened in my life.
Oprah Winfrey

DATE: _____
I am so happy and grateful now that . . .
1. _____
2. _____
3. _____
4. _____

DATE: _____
I am so happy and grateful now that . . .
1. _____
2. _____
3. _____
4. _____

DATE: _____
I am so happy and grateful now that . . .
1. _____
2. _____
3. _____
4. _____

DATE: _____
I am so happy and grateful now that . . .
1. _____
2. _____
3. _____
4. _____

DATE: _____ Week 27 - Week 39

I am so happy and grateful now that . . .

1. _____
2. _____
3. _____
4. _____

DATE: _____

I am so happy and grateful now that . . .

1. _____
2. _____
3. _____
4. _____

DATE: _____

I am so happy and grateful now that . . .

1. _____
2. _____
3. _____
4. _____

Things that touched my heart the most this week:

_____
_____
_____
_____
_____
_____
_____
_____

The Art of Gratitude

We can only be said to be alive in those moments when our hearts are conscious of our treasures.
Thorton Wilder

DATE: _____
I am so happy and grateful now that . . .
1. _____
2. _____
3. _____
4. _____

DATE: _____
I am so happy and grateful now that . . .
1. _____
2. _____
3. _____
4. _____

DATE: _____
I am so happy and grateful now that . . .
1. _____
2. _____
3. _____
4. _____

DATE: _____
I am so happy and grateful now that . . .
1. _____
2. _____
3. _____
4. _____

DATE: _____ Week 27 - Week 39

I am so happy and grateful now that . . .

1. _____
2. _____
3. _____
4. _____

DATE: _____

I am so happy and grateful now that . . .

1. _____
2. _____
3. _____
4. _____

DATE: _____

I am so happy and grateful now that . . .

1. _____
2. _____
3. _____
4. _____

Things that touched my heart the most this week:

_____
_____
_____
_____
_____
_____
_____
_____
_____

The Art of Gratitude

I still miss those I loved who are no longer with me but I find I am grateful for having loved them.
The gratitude has finally conquered the loss.
Rita Mae Brown

DATE: _____
I am so happy and grateful now that . . .

1. _____
2. _____
3. _____
4. _____

DATE: _____
I am so happy and grateful now that . . .

1. _____
2. _____
3. _____
4. _____

DATE: _____
I am so happy and grateful now that . . .

1. _____
2. _____
3. _____
4. _____

DATE: _____
I am so happy and grateful now that . . .

1. _____
2. _____
3. _____
4. _____

Week 27 - Week 39

DATE: _____
I am so happy and grateful now that . . .
1. _____
2. _____
3. _____
4. _____

DATE: _____
I am so happy and grateful now that . . .
1. _____
2. _____
3. _____
4. _____

DATE: _____
I am so happy and grateful now that . . .
1. _____
2. _____
3. _____
4. _____

Things that touched my heart the most this week:
_____
_____
_____
_____
_____
_____
_____
_____
_____

The Art of Gratitude

*I finally realized that being grateful to my body
was key to giving more love to myself.*
Oprah Winfrey

DATE: _____
I am so happy and grateful now that . . .
1. _____
2. _____
3. _____
4. _____

DATE: _____
I am so happy and grateful now that . . .
1. _____
2. _____
3. _____
4. _____

DATE: _____
I am so happy and grateful now that . . .
1. _____
2. _____
3. _____
4. _____

DATE: _____
I am so happy and grateful now that . . .
1. _____
2. _____
3. _____
4. _____

DATE: _____ Week 27 - Week 39

I am so happy and grateful now that . . .

1. _____
2. _____
3. _____
4. _____

DATE: _____

I am so happy and grateful now that . . .

1. _____
2. _____
3. _____
4. _____

DATE: _____

I am so happy and grateful now that . . .

1. _____
2. _____
3. _____
4. _____

Things that touched my heart the most this week:

_____
_____
_____
_____
_____
_____
_____
_____

The Art of Gratitude

Love and gratitude can part seas, move mountains, and create miracles.
Rhonda Byrne

DATE: _____
I am so happy and grateful now that . . .
1. _____
2. _____
3. _____
4. _____

DATE: _____
I am so happy and grateful now that . . .
1. _____
2. _____
3. _____
4. _____

DATE: _____
I am so happy and grateful now that . . .
1. _____
2. _____
3. _____
4. _____

DATE: _____
I am so happy and grateful now that . . .
1. _____
2. _____
3. _____
4. _____

DATE: _____   Week 27 - Week 39

I am so happy and grateful now that . . .

1. _____
2. _____
3. _____
4. _____

DATE: _____

I am so happy and grateful now that . . .

1. _____
2. _____
3. _____
4. _____

DATE: _____

I am so happy and grateful now that . . .

1. _____
2. _____
3. _____
4. _____

Things that touched my heart the most this week:

_____
_____
_____
_____
_____
_____
_____
_____

The Art of Gratitude

The discipline of gratitude is the explicit effort to acknowledge that all I am and have is given to me as a gift of love, a gift to be celebrated with joy.
Henri Nouwen

DATE: _____
I am so happy and grateful now that . . .
1. _____
2. _____
3. _____
4. _____

DATE: _____
I am so happy and grateful now that . . .
1. _____
2. _____
3. _____
4. _____

DATE: _____
I am so happy and grateful now that . . .
1. _____
2. _____
3. _____
4. _____

DATE: _____
I am so happy and grateful now that . . .
1. _____
2. _____
3. _____
4. _____

DATE: _____   Week 27 - Week 39

I am so happy and grateful now that . . .

1. _____
2. _____
3. _____
4. _____

DATE: _____

I am so happy and grateful now that . . .

1. _____
2. _____
3. _____
4. _____

DATE: _____

I am so happy and grateful now that . . .

1. _____
2. _____
3. _____
4. _____

Things that touched my heart the most this week:

_____
_____
_____
_____
_____
_____
_____
_____

The Art of Gratitude

What seems to us as bitter trials are often blessings in disguise.
Oscar Wilde

DATE: _____
I am so happy and grateful now that . . .
1. _____
2. _____
3. _____
4. _____

DATE: _____
I am so happy and grateful now that . . .
1. _____
2. _____
3. _____
4. _____

DATE: _____
I am so happy and grateful now that . . .
1. _____
2. _____
3. _____
4. _____

DATE: _____
I am so happy and grateful now that . . .
1. _____
2. _____
3. _____
4. _____

DATE: _____ Week 27 - Week 39

I am so happy and grateful now that . . .

1. _____
2. _____
3. _____
4. _____

DATE: _____

I am so happy and grateful now that . . .

1. _____
2. _____
3. _____
4. _____

DATE: _____

I am so happy and grateful now that . . .

1. _____
2. _____
3. _____
4. _____

Things that touched my heart the most this week:

_____
_____
_____
_____
_____
_____
_____
_____

The Art of Gratitude

The roots of all goodness lie in the soil of appreciation for goodness.
Dalai Lama

DATE: _____
I am so happy and grateful now that . . .
1. _____
2. _____
3. _____
4. _____

DATE: _____
I am so happy and grateful now that . . .
1. _____
2. _____
3. _____
4. _____

DATE: _____
I am so happy and grateful now that . . .
1. _____
2. _____
3. _____
4. _____

DATE: _____
I am so happy and grateful now that . . .
1. _____
2. _____
3. _____
4. _____

DATE: _____   Week 27 - Week 39

I am so happy and grateful now that . . .
1. _____
2. _____
3. _____
4. _____

DATE: _____

I am so happy and grateful now that . . .
1. _____
2. _____
3. _____
4. _____

DATE: _____

I am so happy and grateful now that . . .
1. _____
2. _____
3. _____
4. _____

Things that touched my heart the most this week:
_____
_____
_____
_____
_____
_____
_____
_____

The Art of Gratitude

The most fortunate are those who have a wonderful capacity to appreciate again and again, freshly and naively, the basic goods of life, with awe, pleasure, wonder, and even ecstasy.
Abraham Maslow

DATE: _____
I am so happy and grateful now that . . .
1. _____
2. _____
3. _____
4. _____

DATE: _____
I am so happy and grateful now that . . .
1. _____
2. _____
3. _____
4. _____

DATE: _____
I am so happy and grateful now that . . .
1. _____
2. _____
3. _____
4. _____

DATE: _____
I am so happy and grateful now that . . .
1. _____
2. _____
3. _____
4. _____

DATE: _____   Week 27 - Week 39
I am so happy and grateful now that . . .
1. _____
2. _____
3. _____
4. _____

DATE: _____
I am so happy and grateful now that . . .
1. _____
2. _____
3. _____
4. _____

DATE: _____
I am so happy and grateful now that . . .
1. _____
2. _____
3. _____
4. _____

Things that touched my heart the most this week:
_____
_____
_____
_____
_____
_____
_____
_____

The Art of Gratitude

Develop an attitude of gratitude, and give thanks for everything that happens to you, knowing that every step forward is a step toward achieving something bigger and better than your current situation.
Brian Tracy

DATE: _____
I am so happy and grateful now that . . .
1. _____
2. _____
3. _____
4. _____

DATE: _____
I am so happy and grateful now that . . .
1. _____
2. _____
3. _____
4. _____

DATE: _____
I am so happy and grateful now that . . .
1. _____
2. _____
3. _____
4. _____

DATE: _____
I am so happy and grateful now that . . .
1. _____
2. _____
3. _____
4. _____

DATE: _____ Week 27 - Week 39

I am so happy and grateful now that . . .

1. _____
2. _____
3. _____
4. _____

DATE: _____

I am so happy and grateful now that . . .

1. _____
2. _____
3. _____
4. _____

DATE: _____

I am so happy and grateful now that . . .

1. _____
2. _____
3. _____
4. _____

Things that touched my heart the most this week:

_____
_____
_____
_____
_____
_____
_____
_____
_____

The Art of Gratitude

There is a calmness to a life lived in gratitude, a quiet joy.
Ralph H. Blum

DATE: _____
I am so happy and grateful now that . . .
1. _____
2. _____
3. _____
4. _____

DATE: _____
I am so happy and grateful now that . . .
1. _____
2. _____
3. _____
4. _____

DATE: _____
I am so happy and grateful now that . . .
1. _____
2. _____
3. _____
4. _____

DATE: _____
I am so happy and grateful now that . . .
1. _____
2. _____
3. _____
4. _____

DATE: _____ Week 27 - Week 39

I am so happy and grateful now that . . .
1. _____
2. _____
3. _____
4. _____

DATE: _____

I am so happy and grateful now that . . .
1. _____
2. _____
3. _____
4. _____

DATE: _____

I am so happy and grateful now that . . .
1. _____
2. _____
3. _____
4. _____

Things that touched my heart the most this week:
_____
_____
_____
_____
_____
_____
_____
_____
_____

The Art of Gratitude

The real gift of gratitude is that the more grateful you are, the more present you become.
Robert Holden

DATE: _____
I am so happy and grateful now that . . .
1. _____
2. _____
3. _____
4. _____

DATE: _____
I am so happy and grateful now that . . .
1. _____
2. _____
3. _____
4. _____

DATE: _____
I am so happy and grateful now that . . .
1. _____
2. _____
3. _____
4. _____

DATE: _____
I am so happy and grateful now that . . .
1. _____
2. _____
3. _____
4. _____

DATE: _____   Week 27 - Week 39

I am so happy and grateful now that . . .

1. _____
2. _____
3. _____
4. _____

DATE: _____

I am so happy and grateful now that . . .

1. _____
2. _____
3. _____
4. _____

DATE: _____

I am so happy and grateful now that . . .

1. _____
2. _____
3. _____
4. _____

Things that touched my heart the most this week:

_____
_____
_____
_____
_____
_____
_____
_____

The Art of Gratitude

Date:_____

Review the last 13 weeks of this journal. List the things you are most grateful to have experienced during this time.

1. _____

2. _____

3. _____

4. _____

5. _____

6. _____

7. _____

8. _____

9. _____

10. _____

11. _____

12. _____

The Art of Gratitude

Date:_____

How do you feel keeping a gratitude journal has impacted the last few months of your life?

_____
_____
_____
_____
_____
_____
_____
_____
_____
_____
_____
_____
_____
_____
_____
_____
_____
_____
_____
_____
_____
_____
_____
_____

The Art of Gratitude

The struggle ends when gratitude begins.
Neale Donald Walsch

DATE: _____
I am so happy and grateful now that . . .
1. _____
2. _____
3. _____
4. _____

DATE: _____
I am so happy and grateful now that . . .
1. _____
2. _____
3. _____
4. _____

DATE: _____
I am so happy and grateful now that . . .
1. _____
2. _____
3. _____
4. _____

DATE: _____
I am so happy and grateful now that . . .
1. _____
2. _____
3. _____
4. _____

DATE: _____   Week 40 - Week 52

I am so happy and grateful now that . . .
1. _____
2. _____
3. _____
4. _____

DATE: _____

I am so happy and grateful now that . . .
1. _____
2. _____
3. _____
4. _____

DATE: _____

I am so happy and grateful now that . . .
1. _____
2. _____
3. _____
4. _____

Things that touched my heart the most this week:

_____
_____
_____
_____
_____
_____
_____
_____
_____

The Art of Gratitude

Living in a state of gratitude is the gateway to grace.
Arianna Huffington

DATE: _____
I am so happy and grateful now that . . .
1. _____
2. _____
3. _____
4. _____

DATE: _____
I am so happy and grateful now that . . .
1. _____
2. _____
3. _____
4. _____

DATE: _____
I am so happy and grateful now that . . .
1. _____
2. _____
3. _____
4. _____

DATE: _____
I am so happy and grateful now that . . .
1. _____
2. _____
3. _____
4. _____

DATE: _____   Week 40 - Week 52

I am so happy and grateful now that . . .

1. _____
2. _____
3. _____
4. _____

DATE: _____

I am so happy and grateful now that . . .

1. _____
2. _____
3. _____
4. _____

DATE: _____

I am so happy and grateful now that . . .

1. _____
2. _____
3. _____
4. _____

Things that touched my heart the most this week:

_____
_____
_____
_____
_____
_____
_____
_____
_____

The Art of Gratitude

*Do not spoil what you have by desiring what you have not;
remember that what you now have was once among
the things you only hoped for.
Epicurus*

DATE: _____
I am so happy and grateful now that . . .
1. _____
2. _____
3. _____
4. _____

DATE: _____
I am so happy and grateful now that . . .
1. _____
2. _____
3. _____
4. _____

DATE: _____
I am so happy and grateful now that . . .
1. _____
2. _____
3. _____
4. _____

DATE: _____
I am so happy and grateful now that . . .
1. _____
2. _____
3. _____
4. _____

DATE: _____　　　　　　Week 40 - Week 52
I am so happy and grateful now that . . .

1. _____
2. _____
3. _____
4. _____

DATE: _____
I am so happy and grateful now that . . .

1. _____
2. _____
3. _____
4. _____

DATE: _____
I am so happy and grateful now that . . .

1. _____
2. _____
3. _____
4. _____

Things that touched my heart the most this week:

_____
_____
_____
_____
_____
_____
_____
_____
_____

The Art of Gratitude

*Not what we say about our blessings, but how we use them,
is the true measure of our thanksgiving.*
W.T. Purkiser

DATE: _____
I am so happy and grateful now that . . .
1. _____
2. _____
3. _____
4. _____

DATE: _____
I am so happy and grateful now that . . .
1. _____
2. _____
3. _____
4. _____

DATE: _____
I am so happy and grateful now that . . .
1. _____
2. _____
3. _____
4. _____

DATE: _____
I am so happy and grateful now that . . .
1. _____
2. _____
3. _____
4. _____

DATE: _____   Week 40 - Week 52
I am so happy and grateful now that . . .
1. _____
2. _____
3. _____
4. _____

DATE: _____
I am so happy and grateful now that . . .
1. _____
2. _____
3. _____
4. _____

DATE: _____
I am so happy and grateful now that . . .
1. _____
2. _____
3. _____
4. _____

Things that touched my heart the most this week:
_____
_____
_____
_____
_____
_____
_____
_____
_____

The Art of Gratitude

Expectation has brought me disappointment. Disappointment has brought me wisdom. Acceptance, gratitude and appreciation have brought me joy and fulfillment.
Rasheed Ogunlaru

DATE: _____
I am so happy and grateful now that . . .
1. _____
2. _____
3. _____
4. _____

DATE: _____
I am so happy and grateful now that . . .
1. _____
2. _____
3. _____
4. _____

DATE: _____
I am so happy and grateful now that . . .
1. _____
2. _____
3. _____
4. _____

DATE: _____
I am so happy and grateful now that . . .
1. _____
2. _____
3. _____
4. _____

Week 40 - Week 52

DATE: _____
I am so happy and grateful now that . . .
1. _____
2. _____
3. _____
4. _____

DATE: _____
I am so happy and grateful now that . . .
1. _____
2. _____
3. _____
4. _____

DATE: _____
I am so happy and grateful now that . . .
1. _____
2. _____
3. _____
4. _____

Things that touched my heart the most this week:

_____
_____
_____
_____
_____
_____
_____
_____
_____

The Art of Gratitude

Gratitude is the memory of the heart.
Jean Baptiste Massieu

DATE: _____
I am so happy and grateful now that . . .
1. _____
2. _____
3. _____
4. _____

DATE: _____
I am so happy and grateful now that . . .
1. _____
2. _____
3. _____
4. _____

DATE: _____
I am so happy and grateful now that . . .
1. _____
2. _____
3. _____
4. _____

DATE: _____
I am so happy and grateful now that . . .
1. _____
2. _____
3. _____
4. _____

DATE: _____   Week 40 – Week 52

I am so happy and grateful now that . . .

1. _____
2. _____
3. _____
4. _____

DATE: _____

I am so happy and grateful now that . . .

1. _____
2. _____
3. _____
4. _____

DATE: _____

I am so happy and grateful now that . . .

1. _____
2. _____
3. _____
4. _____

Things that touched my heart the most this week:

_____
_____
_____
_____
_____
_____
_____
_____

The Art of Gratitude

We think we have to do something to be grateful or something has to be done in order for us to be grateful, when gratitude is a state of being.
Iyanla Vanzant

DATE: _____
I am so happy and grateful now that . . .
1. _____
2. _____
3. _____
4. _____

DATE: _____
I am so happy and grateful now that . . .
1. _____
2. _____
3. _____
4. _____

DATE: _____
I am so happy and grateful now that . . .
1. _____
2. _____
3. _____
4. _____

DATE: _____
I am so happy and grateful now that . . .
1. _____
2. _____
3. _____
4. _____

DATE: _____   Week 40 - Week 52

I am so happy and grateful now that . . .

1. _____
2. _____
3. _____
4. _____

DATE: _____

I am so happy and grateful now that . . .

1. _____
2. _____
3. _____
4. _____

DATE: _____

I am so happy and grateful now that . . .

1. _____
2. _____
3. _____
4. _____

Things that touched my heart the most this week:

_____
_____
_____
_____
_____
_____
_____
_____

The Art of Gratitude

*Some people grumble that roses have thorns;
I am grateful that thorns have roses.*
Alphonse Karr

DATE: _____
I am so happy and grateful now that . . .
1. _____
2. _____
3. _____
4. _____

DATE: _____
I am so happy and grateful now that . . .
1. _____
2. _____
3. _____
4. _____

DATE: _____
I am so happy and grateful now that . . .
1. _____
2. _____
3. _____
4. _____

DATE: _____
I am so happy and grateful now that . . .
1. _____
2. _____
3. _____
4. _____

DATE: _____

Week 40 - Week 52

I am so happy and grateful now that . . .

1. _____
2. _____
3. _____
4. _____

DATE: _____

I am so happy and grateful now that . . .

1. _____
2. _____
3. _____
4. _____

DATE: _____

I am so happy and grateful now that . . .

1. _____
2. _____
3. _____
4. _____

Things that touched my heart the most this week:

_____
_____
_____
_____
_____
_____
_____
_____

The Art of Gratitude

Appreciation is a wonderful thing. It makes what is excellent in others belong to us as well.
Voltaire

DATE: _____
I am so happy and grateful now that . . .
1. _____
2. _____
3. _____
4. _____

DATE: _____
I am so happy and grateful now that . . .
1. _____
2. _____
3. _____
4. _____

DATE: _____
I am so happy and grateful now that . . .
1. _____
2. _____
3. _____
4. _____

DATE: _____
I am so happy and grateful now that . . .
1. _____
2. _____
3. _____
4. _____

DATE: _____ Week 40 - Week 52

I am so happy and grateful now that . . .

1. _____
2. _____
3. _____
4. _____

DATE: _____

I am so happy and grateful now that . . .

1. _____
2. _____
3. _____
4. _____

DATE: _____

I am so happy and grateful now that . . .

1. _____
2. _____
3. _____
4. _____

Things that touched my heart the most this week:

_____
_____
_____
_____
_____
_____
_____
_____
_____

The Art of Gratitude

I would maintain that thanks are the highest form of thought, and that gratitude is happiness doubled by wonder.
GK Chesteron

DATE: _____
I am so happy and grateful now that . . .
1. _____
2. _____
3. _____
4. _____

DATE: _____
I am so happy and grateful now that . . .
1. _____
2. _____
3. _____
4. _____

DATE: _____
I am so happy and grateful now that . . .
1. _____
2. _____
3. _____
4. _____

DATE: _____
I am so happy and grateful now that . . .
1. _____
2. _____
3. _____
4. _____

Week 40 - Week 52

DATE: _____
I am so happy and grateful now that . . .
1. _____
2. _____
3. _____
4. _____

DATE: _____
I am so happy and grateful now that . . .
1. _____
2. _____
3. _____
4. _____

DATE: _____
I am so happy and grateful now that . . .
1. _____
2. _____
3. _____
4. _____

Things that touched my heart the most this week:
_____
_____
_____
_____
_____
_____
_____
_____

The Art of Gratitude

Those who drink richly from the cup of thankfulness find themselves refreshed and their cup refilled.
Skip Prichard

DATE: _____
I am so happy and grateful now that . . .
1. _____
2. _____
3. _____
4. _____

DATE: _____
I am so happy and grateful now that . . .
1. _____
2. _____
3. _____
4. _____

DATE: _____
I am so happy and grateful now that . . .
1. _____
2. _____
3. _____
4. _____

DATE: _____
I am so happy and grateful now that . . .
1. _____
2. _____
3. _____
4. _____

DATE: _____

Week 40 - Week 52

I am so happy and grateful now that . . .

1. _____
2. _____
3. _____
4. _____

DATE: _____

I am so happy and grateful now that . . .

1. _____
2. _____
3. _____
4. _____

DATE: _____

I am so happy and grateful now that . . .

1. _____
2. _____
3. _____
4. _____

Things that touched my heart the most this week:

_____
_____
_____
_____
_____
_____
_____
_____
_____

The Art of Gratitude

*Gratitude is what you feel when you want
what you already have.*
James Clear

DATE: _____
I am so happy and grateful now that . . .
1. _____
2. _____
3. _____
4. _____

DATE: _____
I am so happy and grateful now that . . .
1. _____
2. _____
3. _____
4. _____

DATE: _____
I am so happy and grateful now that . . .
1. _____
2. _____
3. _____
4. _____

DATE: _____
I am so happy and grateful now that . . .
1. _____
2. _____
3. _____
4. _____

DATE: _____ **Week 40 - Week 52**
I am so happy and grateful now that . . .
1. _____
2. _____
3. _____
4. _____

DATE: _____
I am so happy and grateful now that . . .
1. _____
2. _____
3. _____
4. _____

DATE: _____
I am so happy and grateful now that . . .
1. _____
2. _____
3. _____
4. _____

Things that touched my heart the most this week:
_____
_____
_____
_____
_____
_____
_____
_____

The Art of Gratitude

May the work of your hands be a sign of gratitude and reverence to the human condition.
Mahatma Gandhi

DATE: _____
I am so happy and grateful now that . . .
1. _____
2. _____
3. _____
4. _____

DATE: _____
I am so happy and grateful now that . . .
1. _____
2. _____
3. _____
4. _____

DATE: _____
I am so happy and grateful now that . . .
1. _____
2. _____
3. _____
4. _____

DATE: _____
I am so happy and grateful now that . . .
1. _____
2. _____
3. _____
4. _____

DATE: _____

Week 40 - Week 52

I am so happy and grateful now that . . .

1. _____
2. _____
3. _____
4. _____

DATE: _____

I am so happy and grateful now that . . .

1. _____
2. _____
3. _____
4. _____

DATE: _____

I am so happy and grateful now that . . .

1. _____
2. _____
3. _____
4. _____

Things that touched my heart the most this week:

_____
_____
_____
_____
_____
_____
_____
_____

The Art of Gratitude

Date:_____

What are the most impactful things you experienced this year that you are grateful for?

_____
_____
_____
_____
_____
_____
_____
_____
_____
_____
_____
_____
_____
_____
_____
_____
_____
_____
_____
_____
_____
_____
_____
_____
_____
_____

The Art of Gratitude

Date:_____

Think about where you were 52 weeks ago. How far do you feel you have progressed in your personal gratitude journey?

_____
_____
_____
_____
_____
_____
_____
_____
_____
_____
_____
_____
_____
_____
_____
_____
_____
_____
_____
_____
_____
_____
_____
_____
_____
_____

www.ingramcontent.com/pod-product-compliance
Lightning Source LLC
Chambersburg PA
CBHW070117080526
44586CB00013B/1324